Geology Rocks!

Sedimentary Rock

Rebecca Faulkner

Raintree

Chicago, Illinois

Design: Victoria Bevan
and AMR Design Ltd (www.amrdesign.com)
Illustrations: David Woodroffe
Picture Research: Melissa Allison and Mica Brancic
Production: Duncan Gilbert

Originated by Chroma Graphics Pte. Ltd
Printed and bound in China by
South China Printing Company

11 10 09
10 9 8 7 6 5 4 3 2

Library of Congress Cataloging-in-Publication Data:
Faulkner, Rebecca.
  Sedimentary rock : Rebecca Faulkner.
    p. cm. -- (Geology rocks!)
  Includes bibliographical references and index.
  ISBN-13: 978-1-4109-2748-4 (Library binding)
  ISBN-10: 1-4109-2748-2 (Library binding)
  ISBN-13: 978-1-4109-2756-9 (pbk)
  ISBN-10: 1-4109-2756-3 (pbk)
  1. Rocks, Sedimentary--Juvenile literature. 2. Rocks--Analysis--Juvenile
literature. I. Title.
  QE471.F39 2007
  552'.5--dc22
                        2006037173

Acknowledgments
The publishers would like to thank the following for permission to reproduce photographs:

Alamy p. **41**, p. **42** (Dennis Cox), p. **28** (Jon Sparks); Corbis pp. **5 bottom inset, 23, 34, 40**, p. **18 bottom** (Bob Krist), p. **4** (Carmen Redondo), p. **31** (David Muench), p. **12** (Galen Rowell), p. **27** (Jonathan Blair), p. **5** (Karen Su), p. **20** (Naturfoto Honal), pp. **5 top inset, 35** (photocuisine/ Chassenet), p. **25** (Remi Benali), p. **22** (Richard Hamilton Smith), p. **13** (Ron Watts), pp. **5 middle inset, 18 top, 38** (Tom Bean); FLPA p. **16** (Minden Pictures/Jim Brandenburg); GeoScience Features Picture Library pp. **9, 11, 24, 26, 39**; Getty Images p. **15** (Harald Sund), p. **7** (Image Bank), p. **19** (National Geographic), p. **37** (Photographer's Choice), p. **44** (Robert Harding), pp. **30, 43** (Stone); Harcourt Education Ltd. p. **32** (Tudor Photography); istockphoto.com p. **10**, p. **21** (Dean Bergmann); OnAsia Images p. **36** (Hitoshi Katanoda); Science Photo Library p. **29** (Alan Sirulnikoff), p. **33** (Alfred Pasieka), p. **42 inset** (Farrell Grehan)

Cover photograph of rock formation in Antelope Canyon, Arizona, USA reproduced with permission of Masterfile (J.A. Kraulis).

CONTENTS

Any words appearing in the text in bold, **like this**, are explained in the glossary. You can also look out for them in the word bank at the bottom of each page.

ROCKS BECOME ROCKS

Humans have been making use of sedimentary rocks for thousands of years. In the past, early humans used a hard sedimentary rock called flint to make the first tools. Later people used clay to make pottery. Most of the fuels that we use today, such as coal and oil, come from sedimentary rocks.

Every day, rivers all over the world are constantly emptying their contents into the ocean. These rivers not only contain water, they also include lumps of rock, sand, and mud. At the same time tiny **marine organisms**, smaller than the period at the end of this sentence, die and fall to the bottom of the ocean. All this material collects on the ocean floor in layers called **sediment**. Over millions of years, this sediment will form sedimentary rocks.

Rocks from ancient oceans

Chalk is a sedimentary rock that forms on the ocean floor. You can find chalk on land in many parts of the world today, so how did it get there? Over millions of years, ancient oceans have dried up and the rock that formed the ocean floors now appears on the land surface where we see it today.

Ancient civilizations carved huge buildings into sedimentary rock, such as this amazing building in Petra, Jordan.

marine organism plant or animal that lives in the ocean

Sedimentary rocks are also forming on the land around us all the time. Sand on beaches and in deserts will eventually turn into **sandstone,** and mudflats will dry out and harden to form **mudstone.** Many of the rocks you see around you are sedimentary rocks.

You might think that once formed, these rocks will last forever. This is not the case. Just as they take millions of years to form, over millions of years they are broken down. The bits of broken rock move on to create new sedimentary rock.

Find out later
Which sedimentary rock do we eat?

How can rocks tell us about dinosaurs?

Where is the most famous sandstone rock in the world?

You may think these amazing landforms in China look like trees, but they have been created from the sedimentary rock limestone as it has been dissolved and partly washed away by water.

sediment pieces of weathered rock

WHAT'S INSIDE EARTH?

We know that sedimentary rocks begin their life on the surface of Earth, but what happens below? The inside of Earth is made up of different layers, like an onion.

A crust of rocks

The **crust** is like the skin of the onion. It is the thinnest layer and it covers the surface of Earth. This is where all sedimentary rocks are found.

Two crusts

There are two types of crust: continental and oceanic. Continental crust is found beneath the **continents** and can be up to 43.5 miles (70 kilometers) thick. Oceanic crust is found beneath the oceans and is up to 6.2 miles (10 kilometers) thick. It is heavier than continental crust.

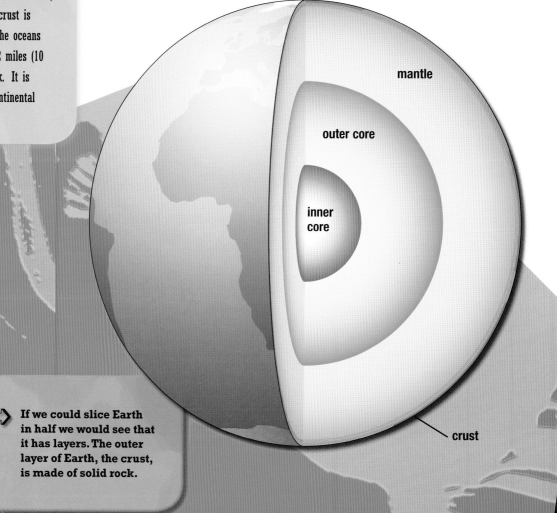

mantle

outer core

inner core

crust

➡ If we could slice Earth in half we would see that it has layers. The outer layer of Earth, the crust, is made of solid rock.

core central layer of Earth
crust thin surface layer of Earth

If we could peel away Earth's crust, the next layer we would find is the **mantle**. This is a thick layer. It starts at the base of the crust and extends 1,800 miles (2,900 kilometers) deep into Earth. The rocks in the mantle are extremely hot—up to 5,400° Fahrenheit (3,000° Celsius). This means that they are partly **molten**.

At the center of Earth, below the mantle, is the **core**. The core can be separated into the outer core and the inner core. The outer core is liquid, and the inner core is solid. We know very little about the core because it is too deep to study.

Fact vs. fiction

A famous book by Jules Verne called *Journey to the Center of the Earth* tells the story of a professor who leads his nephew down a volcano in Iceland to the center of Earth. Be warned though, this is just a story, it could never really happen. Even if we could drill down into the mantle the drill would melt a long time before it reached Earth's core.

↑ In some parts of the Atacama Desert, Chile, Earth's crust is not covered with soil or buildings, so we can see it is made of rock.

mantle hot layer of Earth beneath the crust
molten melted

Does the crust move?

Earth's **crust** is not one solid layer around the **mantle**. It is broken up into huge, moving pieces called **plates**. The plates float like rafts on the mantle below. They move very slowly, up to 4 inches (10 centimeters) per year. The plates are always moving, and they carry the **continents** and oceans with them.

In some places plates are moving towards each other. When this happens one plate may slide under the other and plunge into the mantle below. Here the rock melts. Volcanoes often form along this kind of **plate boundary**, for example in the Andes in South America.

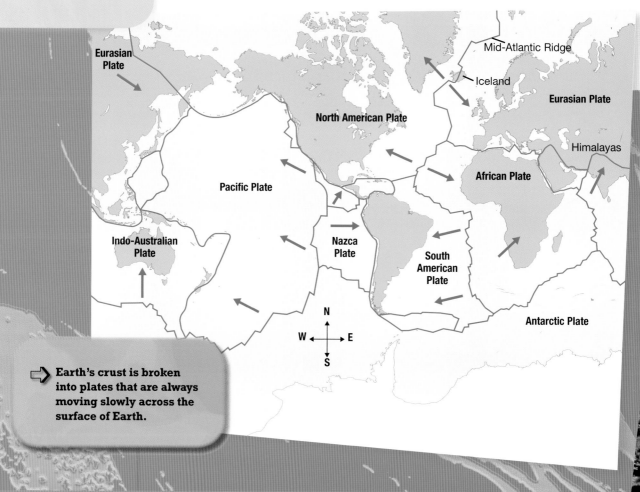

⟹ Earth's crust is broken into plates that are always moving slowly across the surface of Earth.

plate giant, moving piece of crust
plate boundary edge of a plate where one plate meets another

In other places the plates move away from each other. This is usually the case along giant mountain chains on the ocean floor, for example the Mid-Atlantic Ridge. This movement creates a gap (**rift**) between the plates. **Lava** rises up to fill the gap and creates new ocean floor.

Sometimes plates may crash into each other. When this happens the crust gets squashed and folded. This can form huge mountains such as the Himalayas.

Plate tectonics

The slow, constant movement of plates is called **plate tectonics**. Plates meet at plate boundaries. These are also called plate margins.

⬆ This sedimentary rock formation in Mexico has been tilted so that it is nearly vertical. The movement of Earth's plates has caused this.

plate tectonics movement of the plates across Earth
rift gap between two plates

RECYCLING ROCKS

The whole of Earth's crust is made of rock and, if you dig deep enough, you will find rocks everywhere. They are found in high mountain ranges, on the ocean floor, in rivers, in deserts, under the ice at the South Pole, and even in your yard.

Big rocks!

Ayers Rock (Uluru) in Australia is made of the sedimentary rock sandstone. The Rock of Gibraltar off the coast of Spain is made from the sedimentary rock limestone.

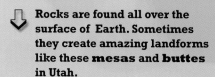

Rocks are found all over the surface of Earth. Sometimes they create amazing landforms like these **mesas** and **buttes** in Utah.

butte eroded tower of sandstone
mesa eroded lump of sandstone with a flat top

What are rocks?

All rocks are made of natural substances called **minerals**. There are more than 4,000 minerals on Earth. Most of these are very rare, and only about 100 are commonly found in rocks. A rock may contain many different minerals. The sedimentary rock **sandstone** contains the minerals quartz, feldspar, and mica. **Limestone** is mainly made up of the mineral calcite, and **mudstone** is made of clay minerals.

Hard rocks!

If a rock contains hard minerals, such as quartz, it will be a hard rock. Sandstone contains lots of quartz, so we know that it is a hard rock.

⬆ Rocks are made up of a mixture of different types of minerals. You can see the individual minerals in this sandstone sedimentary rock.

mineral naturally occurring particle. Rocks are made from lots of minerals.

What types of rock are there?

Earth's **crust** is made up of three types of rock:
- **igneous rock**
- **sedimentary rock**
- **metamorphic rock**.

Each of these types of rock is created in different ways.

Igneous rocks are made from hot runny material called **magma** that is found in the **mantle**. Over millions of years the magma rises up from the mantle. It moves through Earth's crust and cools and hardens to form igneous rock.

Granite

Granite is an igneous rock. It contains the minerals quartz, feldspar, mica, and hornblende, and is usually a pale-colored rock. Different types of granite contain different amounts of the main minerals, so they vary in color from gray to pink.

⇨ **This landform is called a batholith, and it is formed from the igneous rock granite. The softer rocks around it have been eroded by wind and rain to leave this striking rock formation.**

deposition laying down weathered rock in a new place
erosion removal and transportation of weathered rock

Wind and rain attack igneous rocks at Earth's surface, and tiny pieces are broken off and carried by the wind or in rivers. This is called **erosion**. These bits of broken rock are eventually dropped in a new place. This is called **deposition**. Over millions of years the pieces build up to form sedimentary rock.

Metamorphic rocks are formed when high pressure or heat changes igneous or sedimentary rocks. When mountain ranges form, the rocks are squashed and buried under the growing mountains. This means they will experience high pressure, so will change into metamorphic rocks. When hot magma rises below Earth's surface it heats up the surrounding igneous rocks, like baking them in an oven. This causes the rocks to change into metamorphic rocks.

Mud and sand

In areas where bits of mud and clay collect, they form the sedimentary rock **mudstone**. In areas where sand collects, the sedimentary rock **sandstone** forms.

⬆ These sandstone rock formations are made from sand grains that have been deposited here. Over millions of years the sand has gradually turned into rock.

The rock cycle

On Earth there is a never-ending cycle of rock formation, break down (**weathering**), transportation (**erosion**) and settlement in a new place (**deposition**). All these processes make up what is called the **rock cycle**. The materials that make up rocks are constantly recycled.

Earth's surface may seem totally solid but, over millions of years, even the hardest rocks are worn away. When **igneous**, sedimentary, and **metamorphic rocks** are exposed at the surface of Earth, they are attacked by wind and rain. This is called weathering, and over time bits of rock are gradually chipped away.

Wearing away

Weathering and erosion work together over millions of years to lower the surface of the land. These processes create a huge amount of material that will continue its journey through the rock cycle.

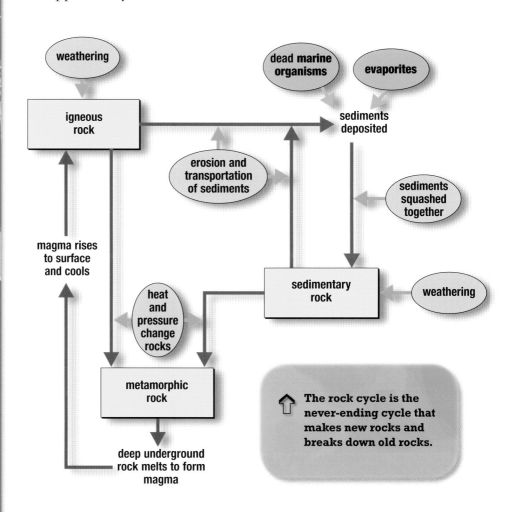

The rock cycle is the never-ending cycle that makes new rocks and breaks down old rocks.

evaporite sedimentary rock formed as water evaporates

Some of the pieces of rock are so small that they are carried away to different places by wind, rivers, or ice. This is called erosion. When the bits of rock can be carried no further, they are dumped in a new place. This is called deposition. Over millions of years deposited **sediment** changes into new rock, and the cycle begins all over again.

In places where **plates** crash into each other, igneous and sedimentary rocks are under intense pressure and heat. Over millions of years they will change into metamorphic rock. In turn, the metamorphic rock may get so hot that it melts and turns into magma. This magma may then rise and solidify to form igneous rock once again.

Old rocks

Earth is at least 4.5 billion years old but, since rocks are continually being destroyed, there are no rocks left that are this old. The oldest rocks that have been found on Earth are in Canada. They are 3.9 billion years old.

⬆ These rocks along the coast of Australia are made of the sedimentary rock limestone. They have been eroded by the sea to form 12 pillars.

SEDIMENTARY ROCKS

Sedimentary rocks can form over millions of years from broken bits of other rocks. All rocks are made of **minerals**. As rocks are attacked by wind, rain, and ice at Earth's surface, some of these minerals are broken off and carried away.

Breaking down rocks

Wind and ice act like sandpaper and scrape at rock until pieces fall off. Wind can then pick up and carry tiny mineral grains and hurl them far across the landscape, sometimes thousands of miles. When rain falls on rocks, some mineral grains in the rock may be dissolved by the water.

Beds of rock

Sediments are laid down in horizontal layers called **beds**. You can tell a rock is sedimentary if you can see the beds in it.

Sand carried by wind and water was laid down in horizontal beds to form this sandstone in the Badlands, South Dakota.

bed horizontal layer of sediment

When the wind dies down, when the ice melts, and when rivers enter the sea, the mineral grains they are carrying are dumped (**deposited**). When this happens the grains are called **sediment**.

Forming sedimentary rock

Over millions of years, beds of sediment are squashed and compacted as new sediment piles on top. This pushes the mineral grains in the sediment closer together. Some mineral grains act like cement and stick the sediment together so that, eventually, sedimentary rock is formed.

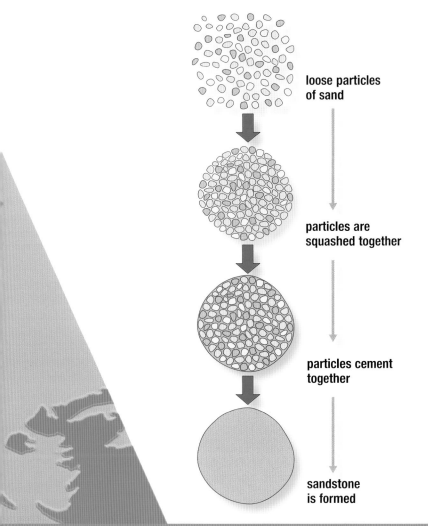

loose particles of sand

particles are squashed together

particles cement together

sandstone is formed

Loose sediment becomes compacted and then cemented over millions of years to form hard sedimentary rock.

If the remains of dead plants or animals fall into the growing pile of **sediment,** they will become part of the sedimentary rock. This is how **fossils** get into rocks. Dinosaur fossils have been found in some rocks, and this is how we know they used to live on Earth.

Some sedimentary rocks contain no fossils, and some contain just one or two. Some rocks contain so many fossils that they are made almost entirely of fossils. **Chalk** is a sedimentary rock made from the shells of tiny **marine organisms** that lived in the ocean millions of years ago. When they died their shells sank to the ocean floor and, over time, changed into rock.

These dinosaur fossils can be seen at Dinosaur National Monument, Colorado.

These huge cliffs are formed from chalk, a type of limestone that is made almost entirely from the shells of millions of marine organisms.

fossil dead remains of a plant or animal found in a rock

Some sedimentary rocks form when water that contains **minerals** evaporates. How do the minerals get into the water in the first place? As water passes over rocks it dissolves some of the minerals. When the water evaporates the minerals are deposited and build up to form rocks such as gypsum and halite (rock salt). These types of rock are called **evaporite** because they form by evaporation.

These are lumps of gypsum. Gypsum is an evaporite, and forms as water evaporates.

Eating rocks!

Did you know that the salt you sometimes add to your food is a sedimentary rock? It is an evaporite called halite, and is commonly known as rock salt. It forms when water evaporates at the edge of shallow lakes or seas in desert areas. Today halite is forming around Salt Lake in Utah, and around the edge of the Dead Sea on the border between Israel and Jordan.

Where are sedimentary rocks formed?

The **minerals** that make up sedimentary rock eventually settle down to rest. This is called **deposition**.

Watery environments

Deposition in rivers mainly takes place in the lower part of the river, near its mouth. This is because the river slows down in its lower part, and so it has less power to carry **sediment**. When it can no longer carry the particles of sediment they drop out of the water, with the heaviest particles being deposited first. If a river bursts its banks and floods out over the valley floor it will deposit pebbles, sand, and silt. Over time these will **lithify** into various sedimentary rocks such as conglomerate, sandstone, or siltstone.

⇩ The fossilized fish in this limestone shows that it formed under water in the deep ocean many millions of years ago. The overlying rocks have since been eroded so that the limestone is now at the surface.

alluvial fan   fan-shaped deposit of sediment, transported by water, found at the bottom of steep slopes

Any sediment still left in the river when it reaches the ocean or a lake will be dumped in a fan-shaped pile of sand called a **delta**. Finer sediment, such as silt and mud, is lighter and so may be carried further into the lake or ocean. Here it will eventually settle and form siltstone and **mudstone**.

When tiny **marine organisms** in the ocean die, their bodies decompose and their shells sink to the ocean floor. These deposits pile up over millions of years and eventually form **limestone**.

Sometimes shallow seas or lakes can evaporate. In places where this happens, **evaporite** will be deposited next to the evaporating sea or lake. If evaporation is intense, the whole of the sea or lake may dry up.

Sandy sediment

When rivers tumble down steep mountainsides and enter flat valleys they dump sandy sediment in fan-shaped deposits called **alluvial fans**. These will harden to form **sandstone**.

This is a huge alluvial fan in Alaska. The deposits will harden over time to form sandstone and other sedimentary rocks.

Icy environments

Glaciers are very slow-moving rivers of ice. They form when snow collects high in the mountains and hardens to form ice. They are found in cold countries, such as Greenland and Iceland, and high in the mountains in places such as Alaska and the Alps in Europe.

When broken rock falls onto glaciers, or is dragged along the ground by glaciers, it becomes embedded in the ice. This rock material will be dumped when the glacier melts. This **sediment** is called **till** or **moraine**. Glaciers can carry large pebbles and boulders, so glacial sediment will eventually **lithify** into sedimentary rocks called **conglomerate**, breccia, or tillite. As the glacier melts, streams will carry fine sediment away.

This is glacial till. We can tell that it was dumped by a melting glacier because the sediment is made up of a jumble of different-sized fragments of rock.

moraine low ridge of rock deposited by a glacier

Windy environments

In deserts, the wind picks up tiny grains of sediment and carries them until the wind drops. This wind-blown sand is deposited in sand dunes. Dunes are the most striking desert landforms, and they can form many different shapes. Sand may only remain on a dune for a short time before the wind picks it up and moves it again. In this way sand may be deposited in different places many times before it becomes buried and eventually turns into rock.

Dust storms

During dust storms, huge amounts of sediment can be transported by the wind from deserts to other regions. When the wind dies down, this sediment will be deposited and over millions of years will form new sedimentary rock.

⬆ Sand and dust are deposited by the wind in deserts. The material in these sand dunes will eventually become cemented to form sandstone.

How can we classify sedimentary rocks?

Sedimentary rocks are classified according to:
- origin and composition
- grain shape
- grain size.

Origin and composition

Sedimentary rocks can be classified into two main groups according to how they formed and what they are made of.

Rocks that are made of bits of other rocks that have been weathered, eroded, and deposited, such as sandstone and mudstone, are called **clastic rocks**.

Rocks that are created when water evaporates, for example **evaporite**, or that form from the dead remains of plants and animals, for example **limestone**, are called **non-clastic rocks**.

Clastic rocks

Clastic rocks are so called because the fragments of rocks and minerals they are made from are called **clasts**.

⬆ This is a microscope image of sandstone. You can see the individual quartz grains have rounded edges, which suggests they were deposited by a river.

clast fragment of rock
clastic rock sedimentary rock that is made from bits of other rock

Grain shape

The shape of the individual **mineral** grains in sedimentary rock determines the **texture** of the rock. The texture of the rock is how it feels. It may feel smooth and greasy, or rough like sandpaper.

Why do grains have different shapes? When mineral grains are carried by wind, water, or ice, they bump into each other. As they do so, the corners of the grains get broken off. The more this happens, the smaller and more rounded the grains become.

Sediment grains carried in glaciers are often angular because the ice protects them from collisions. Grains carried by the wind are able to collide violently many times so they become well rounded. Grains transported by water are usually smooth and polished, with rounded edges.

Sediment grains

Sediment grains can be classified as being very angular, angular, rounded, or well rounded.

Grain shape	What it looks like
very angular	
angular	
rounded	
well rounded	

← During a dust storm, the grains will crash into each other violently many times, resulting in well-rounded grains.

Grain size

Clastic rocks can be grouped according to the size of the individual **mineral** grains that make up the rock. These can vary from microscopic clay particles to huge boulders as big as a house.

Coarse grained rocks are those that contain pebbles more than 0.2 inches (4 millimeters) across. **Conglomerate** is an example of a coarse grained sedimentary rock.

 You can see the large grain size of the minerals in conglomerate.

Rocks containing sand-sized mineral grains ranging from 0.002 to 0.2 inches (0.06 to 4 millimeters) across are described as medium-grained rocks. The sedimentary rock **sandstone** falls into this category. Fine-grained sedimentary rocks contain silt-sized grains, from 0.0002 to 0.002 inches (0.004 to 0.06 millimeters) across. **Siltstone** is a fine-grained sedimentary rock. The grains are just about visible to the bare eye.

Very fine grained sedimentary rocks contain tiny grains of clay, less than 0.0002 inches (0.004 millimeters) across. You cannot see the individual grains in very fine grained rocks without a microscope.

Shale

Shale is an example of a very fine-grained sedimentary rock. It is a type of **mudstone** and is one of the most common sedimentary rocks on Earth.

⬆ Tiny particles of clay are deposited in layers, usually on the bottom of lakes, to form the sedimentary rock shale. It is so fine grained that you cannot see the individual minerals without a microscope.

There are many different types of sedimentary rock, distributed all over the world. They can be divided into groups according to their origin, composition, grain size, and grain shape.

Clastic rocks

Conglomerate

Conglomerate is a coarse grained sedimentary rock formed from pebbles, cobblestones, or boulders that are cemented together with sand. The pebbles often have smooth, rounded edges because they have been deposited by fast-flowing rivers. Conglomerate is a very hard rock and it rarely contains **fossils**.

Breccia and till

Breccia and **till** are similar to conglomerate, but contain sharp-edged pebbles and are deposited by rivers or glaciers on steep mountain slopes.

⬆ The rock outcrops in this desert in Jordan are formed from sandstone.

28

Sandstone

Sandstone is a medium-grained rock that contains a lot of quartz. It is deposited in dry areas such as deserts, and also in river **deltas** and the ocean. Fossils may be found in sandstone rocks. Orthoquartzite is a type of sandstone that consists almost entirely of quartz.

Siltstone

Siltstone is a fine-grained rock deposited in deltas and lagoons. It consists mainly of the **minerals** quartz, feldspar, and mica. Fossils are often found in siltstone.

Mudstone

Mudstone is a very fine-grained rock formed from layers of compacted clay. The tiny clay particles are deposited by very still water in the ocean, lakes, and lagoons. Mudstone feels smooth and not gritty.

Colorful sandstone

Sandstone may be any color, but the most common colors are brown, yellow, and red. The desert areas of the western states are well known for their red sandstone.

Shale is a type of mudstone that often contains fossils. It splits easily into sheets.

Non-clastic rocks

Limestone

Limestone is a sedimentary rock that consists largely of the **mineral** calcite. It often contains many **fossils**. In fact it is rare to not find fossils in limestone, but they may be partly destroyed. It is not surprising that fossils are common in limestone because it is formed in the ocean from the shells and skeletons of dead sea creatures.

Coal

Coal is formed from the dead remains of forests. Millions of years ago, when the forest plants and trees died, they fell to the swampy forest floor and were covered with layers of **sediment**. Over millions of years, as the remains were buried deeper under more and more layers of sediment, they became squashed and turned into coal.

This mountain range in northern Italy is called the Dolomites because the dominant rock type is dolomite, a type of limestone. This rock formed on the floor of an ancient ocean.

coal fossil fuel formed from the dead remains of forest plants

Evaporite

Evaporite is formed when minerals such as gypsum and halite (rock salt) are deposited when water evaporates from lagoons, oceans, and lakes. It is common in desert areas, where evaporation is high, such as the Great Salt Lake in Utah. In places such as this, the high temperatures cause evaporation at the edges of lakes and shallow seas.

⇩ **This region of salt deposits on the bed of a dried-up lake in Death Valley, California, is known as the Devil's Golf Course.**

Travertine

Travertine is a calcite-rich rock that forms as water evaporates around hot springs. Deposits are common in Italy, Turkey, and Greece. The Colosseum in Rome, Italy, is constructed largely of travertine.

How can we identify sedimentary rocks?

You may have seen beautiful and amazing sedimentary rocks in museums, or pictures of them in books, but how would you feel if you actually found one yourself? Would you know what it was?

Every day you see rocks of all shapes and sizes. You can find rocks in your local park, by the sides of roads, or in fields and woods. You can also find rocks all around you as gravestones, steps, on your house, or your school buildings.

It is not always easy to tell if a rock is sedimentary or not. You will need to look at the rock closely and ask yourself some questions.

Look around you

Learning how to identify rocks can be fun, and you can start by looking at rocks in your local area. A lot of the rocks you can see will be sedimentary rocks.

⇨ **This student is examining a piece of sandstone.**

thin section very thin slice of rock mounted on a microscope slide

Can you see any layers in the rock?
Can you break bits off the rock with your hands?
Can you see any **fossils** in the rock?
Can you see any broken bits of shells in the rock?

If the answer to any of these questions is "yes," then the rock is likely to be sedimentary.

When scientists want to find out what type of rock a sample is they take very thin slices of the rock, called **thin sections**. They examine the thin sections under a microscope. When the rocks are magnified in this way, the individual **minerals** they contain can be seen. Scientists can study these minerals and use their knowledge to figure out what kind of rock it is.

The "fizz test"
Experts sometimes use the "fizz test" to determine whether a rock is limestone or not. They drip a small amount of hydrochloric acid onto the rock. If the rock fizzes and a gas is given off, then the rock is a type of limestone.

This is a thin section of **limestone**. By looking at the rock under a microscope scientists can see which minerals it contains.

BUILDINGS AND FUEL

The Pyramids

The Pyramids in Egypt were carved out of limestone more than 3,500 years ago and are still standing today. They had a coating of white limestone on the outside, but this was removed and used for more recent buildings in Cairo.

Now that you know what sedimentary rocks look like, you can look out for how they have been used by people in many different ways. You may have seen **sandstone** buildings in historic cities, but you may not know that the glass in your school windows is also made from sandstone. In this case it has been ground to a powder, mixed with other things, and heated to form glass.

Building stones

Sedimentary rocks have many uses in building work. Sandstone and **limestone** are often used for building because they look beautiful, are readily available, and easy to work with. St. Paul's Cathedral in London and Notre Dame in Paris are made from limestone. The Empire State Building in New York is made of limestone and the **igneous rock** granite.

⇨ This huge limestone statue called the Sphinx can be found near the Pyramids just outside Cairo in Egypt. It has the head of a human and the body of a lion, and has been eroded by the wind for thousands of years.

Shale and **mudstone** are used to make bricks and tiles that can be used in buildings. Limestone is used to make the cement that holds the bricks together. An **evaporite** rock called gypsum is used to make the plaster that makes the inside walls of houses smooth.

Do you know that you even eat sedimentary rocks? Every time you add salt to your food think about where it has come from. Rock salt is called halite and is an evaporite deposit that forms when salt water evaporates. Halite has many other uses in addition to using it to flavor our food. We also put it on roads in icy weather to melt the ice faster.

Blasting rocks!
Getting rocks out of the ground so that we can use them is sometimes very difficult. Explosives are often used in quarries to blast the rock and break it up.

⬇ We add salt to our food. But did you know it is a sedimentary rock?

Fossil fuels

Sedimentary rocks are important sources of **fossil fuels**. We use fossil fuels to heat and light our homes, to power our cars, and to make lots of different types of plastic. Without fossil fuels our lives would be very different.

Coal and **oil** are called fossil fuels because they are made from **fossils** of plants and animals that lived on Earth millions of years ago. When they are burned, energy is released as heat and light.

Coalfields are the remains of huge forests that existed millions of years ago, when the climate was much warmer and wetter than it is now.

Electricity from rocks

Because coal is buried underground, it needs to be extracted from the ground by mining to make it available for use. It can then be burned in power stations to produce electricity, or used for heating homes in coal fires.

Coal is often buried deep underground and has to be mined to **extract** it from Earth. This can be a dangerous job.

extract take out

Coal is mined in countries such as Australia, China, Germany, Russia, the United Kingdom and the United States. Before the discovery of oil, coal was the most important energy resource on Earth. Now it has mostly been replaced by oil and natural gas, so many coal mines have been closed.

Oil is found in sedimentary rocks such as shale. It is formed from the dead remains of plants and animals that fell to the ocean floor and became covered with layers of **sediment**. Over millions of years, as the remains were buried deeper under more layers of sediment, they became squashed and turned into oil.

Oil from rocks

Oil is often found in rocks below the ocean floor, so oil rigs are built in the ocean to get the oil out of the rocks below. The oil is then taken to oil refineries by tankers and pipelines. It is made into gasoline and the other forms of oil that we can use. It is also made into materials, for example plastics.

➡ **The oil that is used to make gasoline is found in shale deposits. Since oil takes millions of years to form, we are using it at a much faster rate than it can be replaced, and it will soon run out.**

INTO THE PAST

In the Grand Canyon in Arizona, the rocks have been laid down in layers. The bottom layer is more than 2 billion years old. The top layer is only about 250 million years old.

As the **beds** in sedimentary rocks are laid down on top of each other over time, they record the passing of time. The oldest layers will be at the bottom of the pile, and more recent layers will be on top. There is a catch, however! **Plate** movements may have tilted the layers, so it is not always easy to tell which rocks are the oldest.

If the layers in a sedimentary rock contain **fossils,** and we know how old the fossils are, we can estimate the age of the rocks. If we find fossils of similar plants or animals in rocks of different ages, we can begin to learn how the plants or animals changed over time.

Sometimes we can find amazing fossils hidden for millions of years in the rocks. They help us determine how life has changed on Earth.

Sedimentary rocks can tell us what the environment and climate were like in the past. The movement of water or wind over loose sand creates ripple marks. When the sand hardens to form sandstone, these ripple marks may be preserved like a footprint in the rock. The ripples show us the direction the water was flowing or the wind was blowing millions of years ago when the rock formed. In the same way, the marks of raindrops falling on soft mud may be preserved as rain prints when the mud hardens into mudstone.

Looking for clues

Geologists are a little like detectives. They look for clues in the rocks that will tell us about what has happened on Earth in the past. You, too, can be a detective. If you find an outcrop of **limestone** containing marine fossils, you know that this was deposited in the ocean. So even though the rock is now on land, you know that the area must have been covered by an ocean at some time in the past.

⬆ These ripple marks are found in solid sedimentary rock. They formed when wind or water moved over the loose **sediment** before it became **lithified**.

Sedimentary Landforms

Sedimentary rock forms dramatic and unusual landforms all around the world.

Sandstone and salt

Dramatic **sandstone** landforms are common in deserts, where the rocks have been eroded by wind over millions of years into weird and wonderful sculptures.

The most famous sandstone landform in the world is Ayers Rock in the desert of central Australia. It is officially called Uluru. This huge lump of rock formed about 500 million years ago as sand was deposited on the floor of an ancient ocean that once covered the whole area. The rock has since been pushed up by Earth movements and eroded to create the form you see today.

Ayers Rock

Ayers Rock is the second largest rock in the world. The largest rock is Mount Augustus, also in Australia. It is over 2,350 feet (700 meters) high.

⬆ Ayers Rock (Uluru) in central Australia is made of sandstone and stands almost 1,150 feet (350 meters) tall and 6 miles (10 kilometers) wide.

The dramatic **mesa** and **butte** landforms in deserts, such as Monument Valley in Utah, are heavily eroded lumps and towers of sandstone that stick up from the desert floor. Natural arches, such as Rainbow Bridge, also in Utah, are further examples of heavily eroded sandstone formations.

Salt flats are created in desert areas where lakes have evaporated and left salt deposits. These can form huge flat plains, such as the Salar de Uyuni in Bolivia, which covers an area of 4,000 square miles (10,000 square kilometers). The deposits of gypsum and halite can be up to 20 feet (6 meters) deep in the middle.

Rainbow Bridge

Rainbow Bridge in Utah, is the largest natural arch in the world. It is almost 295 feet (90 meters) long and stands almost 280 feet (85 meters) above the desert floor. It is wide enough to drive a car across.

⬇ Sedimentary rocks can be eroded into spectacular landforms. Eventually, over millions of years, this arch will collapse and the minerals will be transported elsewhere to form new rock.

Limestone landscapes

Amazing landforms can form in **limestone** areas. The main reason for this is because the calcite in limestone dissolves in rainwater. Limestone scenery is called **karst** scenery and can be found in areas as different as China, Cuba, and the United Kingdom. The name karst comes from a limestone area in former Yugoslavia. It means bare and waterless.

When water flows across flat-lying areas of limestone called **limestone pavements,** it seeps through cracks and gradually dissolves the rock below the surface. This creates many interesting underground landforms such as passages and caves.

Limestone caves

The largest limestone cave system in the world is over 311 miles (500 kilometers) long and can be found in Mammoth Cave National Park in Kentucky. The longest stalactite in the world is thought to be in a limestone cave in County Clare, Ireland. It is over 20 feet (6 meters) long.

⬇ **This dramatic scenery is formed through the action of water on the sedimentary rock limestone.**

⬆ **Stalactites and stalagmites form in limestone caves where water seeps through the overlying rocks, dissolving calcite as it does so. As it drips into the cave it forms these amazing features.**

karst limestone scenery

The calcite-rich water drips from the cave ceilings to form **stalactites** that look like rocky icicles. **Stalagmites** also grow up from the cave floor and sometimes join up with the stalactites to form long columns of rock.

Sometimes the caves and passages become too big to support the overlying rock, and so the limestone collapses to form gorges and steep-sided limestone pinnacles.

Furry water?

Take a look in your tea kettle, coffee pot, or other place you frequently have water. If you live in a limestone area you may see a furry deposit inside. This forms because the water in limestone areas contains a lot of calcite. Water containing calcite is called hard water.

⇩ **Underneath this limestone pavement in Yorkshire, UK, there are many underground passages and caves.**

You can find sedimentary rocks all over Earth's surface. They are being created and destroyed all the time and form many dramatic landforms, from steep-sided pinnacles to vast stretches of salt flats.

There are many different types of sedimentary rock, depending on how they form. Some are created from the broken bits of other rocks. **Weathering** processes continually attack rocks and manage to break up even the toughest of rocks. These bits of broken rock are then carried away by rivers, ice, and wind and are deposited in **deltas**, lakes, or the ocean. You can often see this **sediment** on the move, either gliding along in rivers or flying through the air in dust storms. The sediment piles up over time, until eventually it **lithifies** to form sedimentary rock.

Other sedimentary rocks form as the shells and skeletons of tiny **marine organisms** collect on the sea floor when they die. **Evaporites** form as water evaporates from lakes and shallow seas in deserts, leaving behind a crust of **mineral** salts.

We have used sedimentary rocks throughout our history, and still use them today. We use them for building, for fuel, and even for food.

We use salt to flavor and preserve our food. The Dead Sea on the border between Israel and Jordan contains 10 times as much salt as ordinary seawater.

FIND OUT MORE

Books

Farndon, John. *Rocks and Minerals*. New York: Dorling Kindersley, 2005.

Harman, Rebecca. *Earth's Processes: Rock Cycles*. Chicago: Heinemann Library, 2006.

Storey, Rita. *Rocks and Stones*. North Mankato, MN: Smart Apple Media, 2007.

Using the Internet

Explore the Internet to find out more about sedimentary rock. You can use a search engine, such as www.yahooligans.com, and type in keywords such as:
- karst
- mesa
- fossils

Websites

These websites are useful starting places for finding out more about geology:

Mineralogical Society of America: www.minsocam.org

Rocks for Kids: www.rocksforkids.com

Search tips

There are billions of pages on the Internet so it can be difficult to find exactly what you are looking for. These search tips will help you find websites more quickly:
- Know exactly what you want to find out about first.
- Use two to six keywords in a search, putting the most important words first.
- Be precise. Only use names of people, places, or things.

GLOSSARY

alluvial fan fan-shaped deposit of sediment, moved by water, found at the bottom of steep slopes

bed horizontal layer of sediment

butte eroded tower of sandstone

chalk sedimentary rock made from sea shells

clast fragment of rock

clastic rock sedimentary rock that is made from pieces of other rock

coal fossil fuel formed from the dead remains of forest plants

conglomerate coarse grained sedimentary rock

continent large land mass

core central layer of Earth

crust thin surface layer of Earth

delta fan-shaped pile of sediment formed where a river meets the ocean or a lake

deposition laying down weathered rock in a new place

erosion removal and transportation of weathered rock

evaporite sediment left behind as water evaporates

extract take out

fossil dead remains of a plant or animal found in a rock

fossil fuel fuel such as coal or oil that is made from fossils

glacier slow moving river of ice

granite type of igneous rock

igneous rock rock formed from magma either underground or at Earth's surface

karst irregular limestone scenery

lava name for magma when it reaches the surface of Earth

limestone sedimentary rock made of calcite

limestone pavement flat area made up of jointed blocks of limestone

lithified turned into rock

magma molten rock from the mantle

mantle hot layer of Earth beneath the crust

marine organism plant or animal that lives in the ocean

mesa eroded lump of sandstone with a flat top

metamorphic rock rock formed when igneous or sedimentary rocks are changed by heat or pressure

mineral naturally occurring particle. Rocks are made from minerals.

molten melted

moraine low ridge of rock deposited by a glacier

mudstone sedimentary rock formed from mud

non-clastic rock sedimentary rock that is formed either when water evaporates or from fossils

oil fossil fuel formed from the dead remains of plants and animals

plate giant, moving piece of crust

plate boundary edge of a plate where one plate meets another

plate tectonics movement of the plates across Earth

rift gap between two plates

rock cycle unending process of rock formation and destruction

sandstone sedimentary rock formed from pieces of sand

sediment pieces of weathered rock

siltstone fine grained sedimentary rock

stalactite thin icicle-shaped lump of rock that forms as water drips down from cave ceilings

stalagmite short, stubby column of rock that forms when water drips onto a cave floor and evaporates

texture how something feels

thin section very thin slice of rock mounted on a microscope slide

till rock material carried and deposited by a glacier

weathering break down of rock by wind and rain

INDEX